A HOUSE IN THE SKY

AND OTHER UNCOMMON ANIMAL HOMES

Steve Jenkins

Illustrated by Robbin Gourley

Charlesbridge

For Robbin—S. J.

For Hannah, Luke, and Jeff—the best co-inhabitants—and to all the critters who dwelled with us: dog, cats, frog, hamsters, rabbits, and fish—R. G.

Text copyright © 2018 by Steve Jenkins
Illustrations copyright © 2018 by Robbin Gourley
All rights reserved, including the right of reproduction in whole or in part in any form. Charlesbridge and colophon are registered trademarks of Charlesbridge Publishing, Inc.

Published by Charlesbridge
85 Main Street
Watertown, MA 02472
(617) 926-0329
www.charlesbridge.com

Library of Congress Cataloging-in-Publication Data
Names: Jenkins, Steve, 1952– author. | Gourley, Robbin, illustrator.
Title: A house in the sky/Steve Jenkins; illustrated by Robbin Gourley.
Description: Watertown, MA: Charlesbridge, [2018]
Identifiers: LCCN 2016053960 (print) | LCCN 2017005155 (ebook) | ISBN 9781580897808 (reinforced for library use) | ISBN 9781632896032 (ebook) | ISBN 9781632896049 (ebook pdf)
Subjects: LCSH: Animals—Habitations—Juvenile literature. | Animal behavior—Juvenile literature.
Classification: LCC QL756.J46 2018 (print) | LCC QL756 (ebook) | DDC 591.56/4—dc23
LC record available at https://lccn.loc.gov/2016053960

Printed in China
(hc) 10 9 8 7 6 5 4 3 2 1

Illustrations done in watercolor
Display type set in Canvas 3D
Text type set in P22 Mayflower and Grenadine
Color separations by Colourscan Print Co Pte Ltd, Singapore
Printed by 1010 Printing International Limited in Huizhou, Guangdong, China
Production supervision by Brian G. Walker
Designed by Susan Mallory Sherman

ANIMALS, like people, often need a cozy place to sleep, a hideaway for escaping danger, or a safe place to raise a family.

They need a house.

Here is a house in the treetops.

The **tree-kangaroo** spends most of its life high above the forest floor, and even sleeps curled up in the branches of a tree.

A house can be under the ground . . .

A **badger** excavates its burrow with powerful claws. It makes a new den often, and it may sleep in a different home every night.

... or suspended above it.

The **reed warbler** hangs its nest from reeds or grass, keeping it safe from danger.

Some houses are made of bubbles . . .

A **Siamese fighting fish** takes a gulp of air and then blows it back out. It does this over and over again, creating a floating nest made of bubbles to protect its babies.

. . . and others are made of clay.

A pair of **red ovenbirds** constructs a nest of mud and plant fibers. The finished shelter looks like an old-fashioned baker's oven, and keeps the birds and their chicks snug and warm.

This house is made of sticks.

A **beaver** family works to fashion a lodge from sticks and mud. When finished, the house has an underwater entrance and a cozy chamber that's high and dry.

And this house is made of stone.

With its tough teeth, the **rock-boring urchin** chews into solid rock or coral. The urchin may spend its entire life safe in the pit it has gnawed into the seafloor.

Here is a house in a hole.

When a **burrowing owl** finds an abandoned
prairie dog den, it moves right in.

Here is a house in a shell.

Wherever it goes, the **box turtle** takes its house along. If danger threatens, the turtle pulls its head, legs, and tail inside its shell, then clamps the shell closed.

Look up—a house in the sky !

The **common swift** spends months at a time in the air, never touching down. It eats, drinks, and sleeps on the wing.

A house can be found . . .

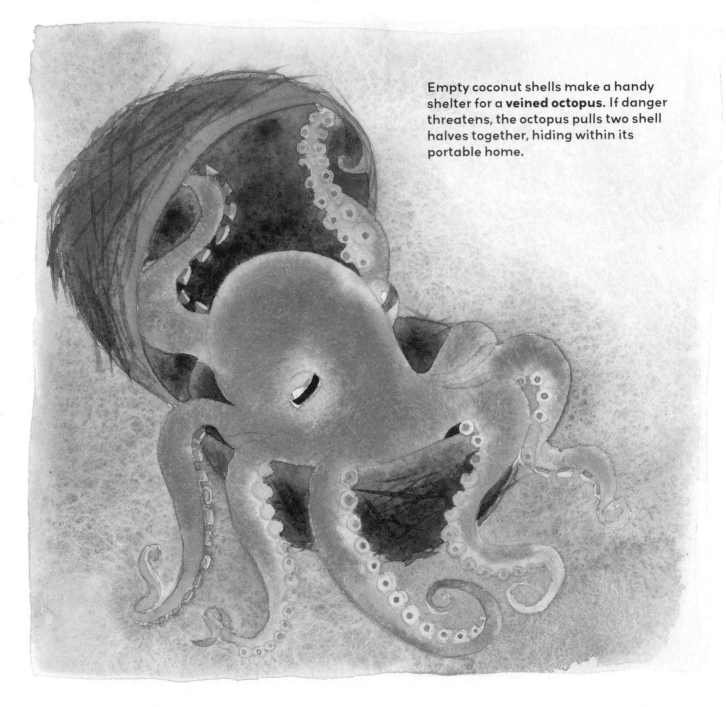

Empty coconut shells make a handy shelter for a **veined octopus**. If danger threatens, the octopus pulls two shell halves together, hiding within its portable home.

. . . or built piece by piece.

Until it hatches and flies away, a **caddis fly larva** lives on the bottom of a lake or stream, wrapped in a silken cocoon. It attaches pebbles or sticks to its temporary home to discourage predators.

This house is borrowed . . .

A **hermit crab** finds an empty seashell and crawls inside. After a while, the crab outgrows its borrowed house and has to search for a bigger shell.

. . . and this house is fit for a queen.

Some **termite** colonies erect tall mounds of earth that can include hundreds of rooms and millions of insects. The queen, the most important member of the colony, lives in a special chamber in the basement.

Look! This house is made to impress . . .

To lure a mate, the male **satin bowerbird** weaves a nest of sticks and festoons it with shells, stones, bottle caps, and other treasures. Bowerbirds will decorate with just about any object they can carry, as long as it is blue.

. . . while this house is made to protect.

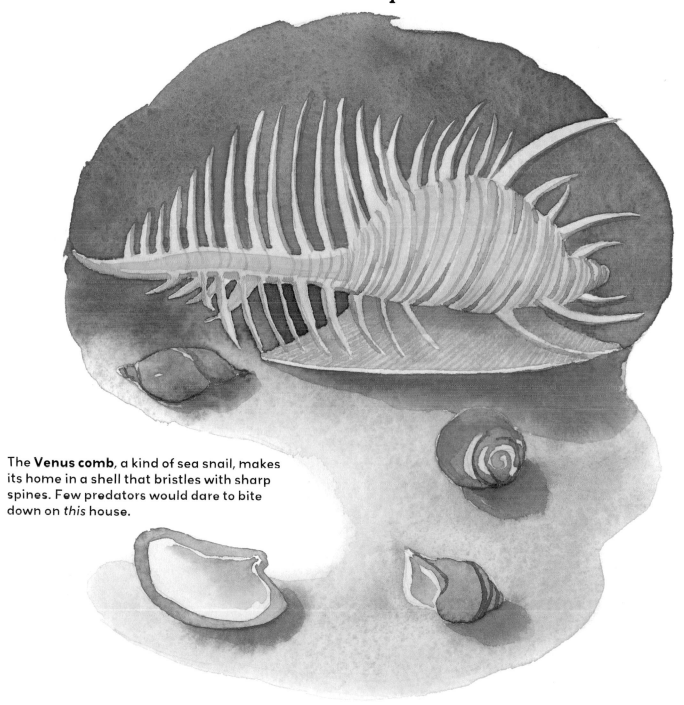

The **Venus comb**, a kind of sea snail, makes its home in a shell that bristles with sharp spines. Few predators would dare to bite down on *this* house.

Who ever heard of a house on a whale?

Whale barnacles cruise the seas attached to their companion, a gray whale. The barnacles don't hurt the whale—they're just along for the ride.

Or a house in my house?

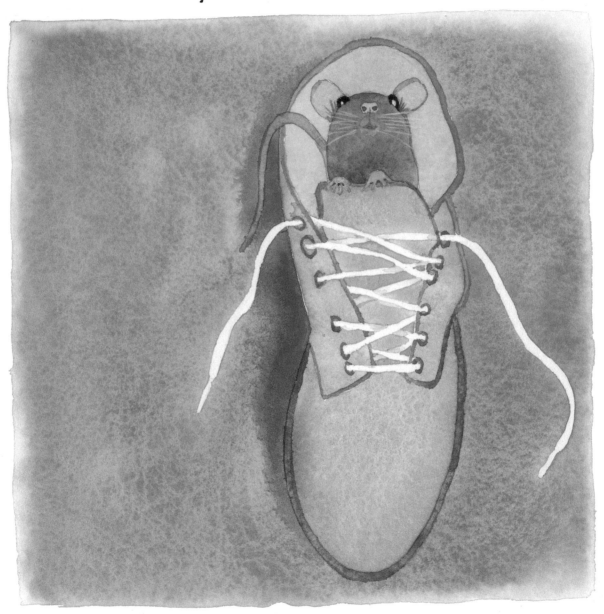

A **house mouse** may build its nest in the walls
of a human's house. Or it may choose a closet,
a drawer—even an old shoe.

A house can even be inside a book!

The larva of a **Mexican book beetle** gnaws through the cover and pages of a book. The beetle lives inside the book until it becomes an adult. Then it chews its way out and flies away.

Houses can be just about anywhere.

A hollow tree stump, a storm drain, or the attic of a building—a **raccoon's** house is anywhere that feels safe.

Here is a house for you!

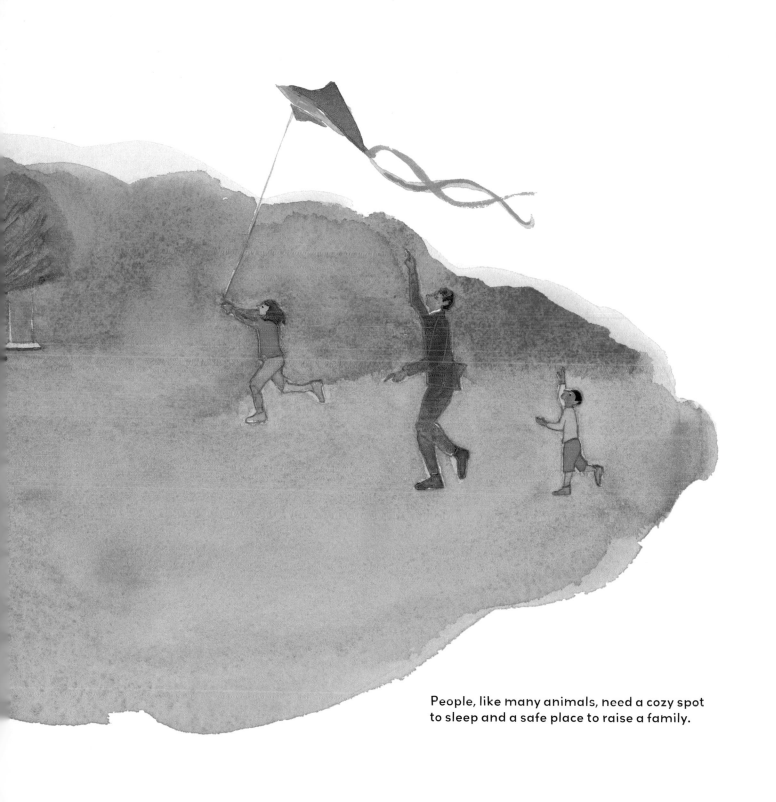

People, like many animals, need a cozy spot
to sleep and a safe place to raise a family.

Tree-kangaroos are marsupials—females nurture their babies in a pouch. These kangaroos are about as big as a medium-size dog. They move awkwardly on the ground, but in the trees they are agile and graceful. They live in the tropical rain forests of New Guinea and northern Australia, where they graze on leaves and fruit.

The **badger** inhabits the grasslands of North America, Europe, Asia, and Africa. Its burrow, which often contains a maze of tunnels, is called a sett. Badgers eat insects, rodents, frogs, birds, and other small animals. They can grow to 3 feet (91 centimeters) in length.

The **reed warbler** builds its nest in the marshes of Europe and Asia. This songbird is about 7 inches (18 centimeters) long and feeds on insects, seeds, and berries. A female reed warbler weaves her nest from reeds and grass and lines it with spiderwebs, animal fur, and soft plant fibers.

Siamese fighting fish are found in rivers, lakes, and rice paddies in Southeast Asia. They are about 2.5 inches (6.5 centimeters) long and feed on insects and small aquatic animals. Siamese fighting fish are often kept as pets, but males will fight each other if two of them are placed in the same aquarium.

Red ovenbirds live in eastern South America. They construct a house made of mud and plant fibers and often attach it to a tree branch or telephone pole. These birds are about 8 inches (20 centimeters) long and feed on insects and grubs.

Beavers construct their house, or lodge, in a lake or pond. The house has an underwater entrance and a dry chamber inside. If necessary, beavers will make their own pond. With their sharp teeth, they cut down trees and use them to block a stream, filling gaps in their dam with sticks and mud. Beavers can weigh as much as 70 pounds (32 kilograms). They eat leaves, bark, roots, and water plants.

The **rock-boring urchin** lives in the shallow waters of the Indian Ocean and western Pacific Ocean. It bores holes in the rocky seafloor with teeth that continue to grow throughout its life. Including its spines, this urchin is about 3 inches (8 centimeters) across. It feeds on algae and coral polyps.

The **burrowing owl** nests in the prairies of North and South America. It finds a burrow made by a prairie dog or other burrowing animal and moves in. Burrowing owls are about 9 inches (23 centimeters) long. They hunt small mammals and insects.

The common **box turtle** can be found in the fields and forests of the eastern United States and Mexico. Its diet includes insects, worms, fruit, and seeds. A box turtle can reach 8 inches (20 centimeters) in length, and it may live more than 100 years.

The **common swift** spends its life in the air, landing only to raise its young. Common swifts are about 6.5 inches (16.5 centimeters) long. They are acrobatic fliers, catching and eating mosquitoes and other airborne insects. These birds live throughout Europe and Asia, migrating to southern Africa in cold weather.

The **veined octopus**, also known as the coconut octopus, lives on sandy seafloors in the Indian Ocean and southwestern Pacific Ocean, where there are few places to hide. A coconut-shell house helps protect it from predators. Including its arms, this octopus is about 6 inches (15 centimeters) long. It hunts shrimp, crabs, and fish.

A **caddis fly larva**—the immature form of the insect—spins a silken cocoon and attaches pebbles, sticks, or bits of water plants to it. This makes the cocoon more difficult to spot and armors it against predators. Caddis flies are found in streams and rivers throughout much of the world. The larvae are typically about three quarters of an inch (2 centimeters) long. As adults, these insects resemble small moths.

Hermit crabs are found in all of the world's oceans. The smallest can be the size of a Ping-Pong ball, and the largest are about as big as a softball. A hermit crab can only grow as large as the snails that live in the same area—otherwise they won't be able to fit into an abandoned shell. Hermit crabs will eat just about anything, including plants, fish, worms, and dead animals.

Mound-building **termites** live in Africa, Australia, and South America, where their colonies can include millions of insects. Their mounds are made of mud mixed with saliva and termite droppings and can be as tall as a two-story house. Soldier termites guard the mound, and worker termites keep it clean and take care of the young. Most of the termites are about half an inch (1.25 centimeters) long, but the queen, whose only job is to lay eggs, can be the size of an adult human's finger.

The male **satin bowerbird** builds its elaborate bower, or nest, in the forests of eastern Australia. A bowerbird's diet consists of fruit, leaves, seeds, and insects. At 12 inches (30 centimeters) long, the male satin bowerbird is a little larger than the female.

The **Venus comb** is a type of sea snail. It lives in warm, shallow water in the Indian Ocean and western Pacific Ocean. It feeds on snails and clams by scraping through their shells with hundreds of tiny teeth, then eating the creatures inside. The spines on the Venus comb protect the snail from predators and keep it from sinking into the seafloor.

Whale barnacles swim freely in the ocean when young, but eventually they attach themselves to something solid—such as a rock, pier, or boat—and grow a hard, protective shell. Whale barnacles are found only on the skin of the gray whale, which may be home to thousands of these hitchhikers, each about the size of a chicken egg. As the whale swims, the barnacles filter and eat algae and plankton from the water.

The **house mouse** often makes its home in human houses, schools, and offices—anyplace where there is food and a spot to make a nest. Mice find a snug nook and line it with shredded paper, cloth, or plant fibers. These rodents are about 3 inches (7.5 centimeters) long. In the wild they eat plants, worms, and insects. Mice that live with humans will eat almost any food they find.

The **Mexican book beetle** is not much larger than the head of a pin. In its larval stage it looks like a tiny caterpillar. In warm and humid climates, the larva causes damage by boring through a book's cover and pages. When it becomes an adult, the beetle chews through the book's spine and flies away to lay eggs on other books, repeating the cycle.

Raccoons are native to North America but have also become common in Europe and Asia. They live in farmlands, towns, and cities, as well as in the wild. Raccoons eat fruit, seeds, insects, frogs, and other small animals. In towns and cities, they consume any human food they can find and are notorious for overturning garbage cans to feast on scraps.